Contents

Introduction

Communication is the process of passing on information. When people talk to each other they are communicating. We also communicate by smiling, frowning and other expressions. The way we move is also a form of communication.

We use words that we learn when we are small children and we also write down our thoughts and ideas. The development of writing was very important because it meant that messages could be sent to people far away and that ideas could be written down and not forgotten. The invention of printing was important, too, because it allowed many copies of a message to be made. In this way many people could read the latest news or story.

Sending messages today

Modern **scientists** have discovered many ways to communicate, or send messages, over long distances. The telephone lets us speak to people who are far away. Radio enables us to hear messages and music from a distant place. With television, we can see events happening in other countries. **Satellites** flying high in the sky pass messages from one country to another at great speed. **Computers** can be used to store information on many subjects. These computers can even be connected to the telephone, so that information can be sent from one computer to another. Using telephones, radio, television and computers in this way is called **telecommunications**.

The story of discovery

Some inventions came about by chance. The telephone was developed because a piece of equipment was knocked accidentally and the sound of the knock was transmitted to the next room. This showed the alert inventor that sounds could be sent along electrical wires. The existence of **radio waves** was first forecast by a scientist using nothing more than a pencil and pad to make mathematical calculations. Later scientists discovered that these radio waves were real.

However, most discoveries are made

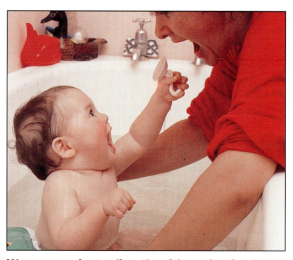

We communicate directly with each other by speech, facial expressions and movements. A baby learns to talk by listening to adults and copying the sounds they make. By the time this baby is ten, he will be able to use thousands of words.

only after many careful **experiments**. Tests are made to see if an idea is correct, and there may be many failures before the problem is solved.

Putting ideas into practice

The way in which scientific ideas can be put to practical use is called **technology**. Modern inventors are quick to make use of scientific discoveries. When scientists first discovered electricity, it had no obvious use. However, within a very short time, it had been used to make the telegraph, the first means of sending messages quickly over long distances. Now electricity is used in almost all communications. In the same way, when computers were first developed many people thought that they would be of little use. One expert at the time thought that no more than six computers would be needed in the whole of Britain! Now there are millions of computers, being used for more and more kinds of tasks. The modern world has come to rely on the many inventions that scientists have made possible. The story of some of those scientists and inventors is told in this book.

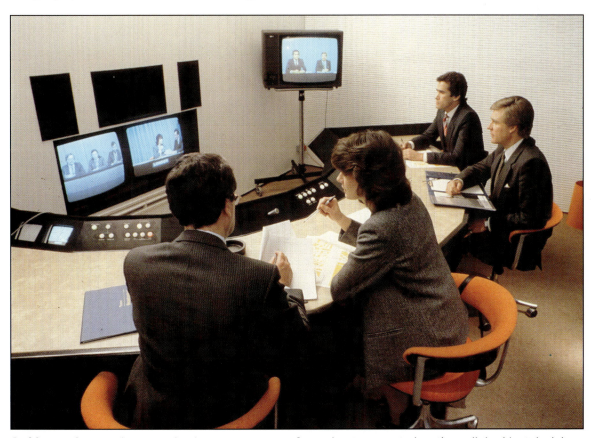

A videoconference is a meeting between groups of people at separate locations, linked by television. The people can see and hear each other even though they may be in different parts of the world.

The alphabet and writing

Human beings are the only animals that make a permanent record of their communications. Today we have many ways of recording a communication. We can write it down, make a sound recording or make a visual recording. Primitive people started by simply writing down the sounds of their language. Words are not always written down using lettershapes. The earliest writing used pictures to represent words. The Sumerian people, who lived in the country now called Iraq about 5500 years ago, were the first to write down their language using pictures called **pictographs**. Each pictograph represented one word.

About 5000 years ago, the ancient Egyptians also used a kind of picture language made up of **hieroglyphs** to write on their tombs and temples. The Egyptian hieroglyphs were more useful than Sumerian pictographs because a hieroglyph could stand for a sound or

Writing in pictures. The first written languages used pictures, called pictographs, to represent words. This tablet was made about 5000 years ago by the Sumerian people.

syllable as well as for a complete word. Some languages are still written in pictographs today. The Chinese and Japanese use picture-like symbols, called **characters**. Each character stands for a whole meaning or sound.

The first writing

About 5000 years ago, the Sumerians and their neighbours the Babylonians started using a type of writing called **cuneiform**. The earlier pictographs were simplified so that they could be made by pressing a sharpened stick into blocks of wet clay. The stick, called a stylus, made wedge-shaped marks that stood for words. The word 'cuneiform' means 'wedge-shaped'. Cuneiform was easy and quick to write and the wet clay with cuneiform writing on it could be dried and kept as a permanent record.

Cuneiform still used symbols for complete words. This was not as useful as writing that used an **alphabet** because there were so many signs to remember. An alphabet is a set of signs each of which stands for a simple sound. These sounds can be combined to make any word, so there is no need to remember the sign for every word.

The alphabet

The first alphabet was used about 3200 years ago at Ugarit in Syria. This used 32 letters standing for single sounds. The Ugarit alphabet is the ancestor of

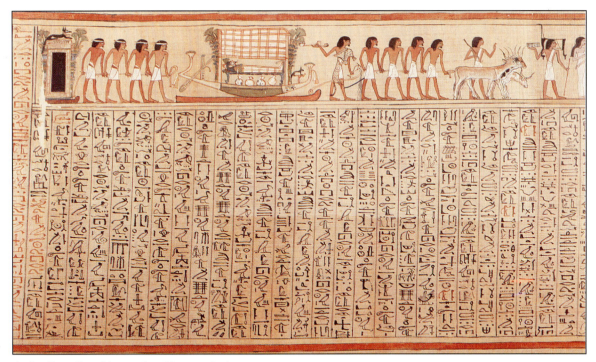

▲ **An Egyptian biography**. The symbols, or heiroglyphs, on this ancient Egyptian scroll describe what will happen to the soul of an important person, Ani, from the time of his death to arrival in heaven. The Egyptians wrote on papyrus, a material made from reeds. This scroll is over 3000 years old.

the modern European alphabet. Its use was spread around the Mediterranean Sea and the Middle East by the Phoenicians. They were great traders who lived on the eastern shore of the Mediterranean and who travelled widely.

The Ugarit alphabet was adopted in many countries. In the east it gradually changed to become Aramaic, from which the Indian, Persian, Arabic and Hebrew alphabets developed. In the west, the Greeks improved the Ugarit alphabet by adding extra letters. Then the Romans took the Greek alphabet and changed it slightly. This is the alphabet

Wedge-shaped marks were used in cuneiform writing, a simplified version of Sumerian pictographs. The symbols were quick and easy to write.

that developed into the alphabet used in modern western European languages. The Russian alphabet, called Cyrillic, also comes from the Greek alphabet and has similar letter forms.

The invention of printing

The most common way of storing written records is in a book. The earliest books were written by hand. People called scribes spent their lives copying the words from one book to produce another. It was slow work and the books were very precious.

Printing began in China over 3000 years ago. It made the production of books much faster. Instead of writing on paper, or **printing** the Chinese cut letters into a stone **block**. The block was then covered with ink and pressed onto paper.

In this way, many copies could be made from one image. The Chinese made the earliest-known printed book in the year 868. It was about the life of the great religious teacher Buddha. In 1040 a Chinese printer called Pi Sheng invented a better system of printing that used small blocks engraved with individual characters.

Printing in Europe was not so advanced and the Chinese methods of printing separate letters were not known. Around 1100 blocks were used to make playing cards and books of pictures with few words.

Johannes Gutenberg

Eventually, in about 1445, Johannes Gutenberg, a German craftsman who lived in Mainz, worked out how to use a separate small block for each letter. This made it possible to print books that had always been written out by hand before. Gutenberg arranged the tiny blocks, called **moveable type**, into words and made lines of words. He used an old wine press as a **printing press**, to press the paper onto the inked type. Gutenberg was the first person to use this process on a large scale.

The first large book to be printed by Gutenberg using this kind of moveable type was a Bible in 1456. It is called the Gutenberg Bible and copies still exist today. By the time of Gutenberg's death in 1468, printing had become widespread in Germany.

The father of modern printing. Johannes Gutenberg created the first real printing press in the 1400s. By making it easier to produce books, Gutenberg helped to spread knowledge around the world.

A hand-operated printing press in the 1500s produced about 300 printed sheets a day.

William Caxton

In 1476, William Caxton, the first English printer, started a printing works in London. He was the son of a London cloth merchant and he had learned about printing in 1470 during a journey to Cologne in Germany. When he returned to London he spent all his money on a printing press, which he set up near Westminster Abbey. In 15 years, he printed 94 different books.

However, Caxton was more than a printer. He translated 20 of the books that he printed from foreign languages. Caxton's work brought about many changes in people's lives. In the 1400s, there were many different forms of English spoken around the country and Caxton had to decide which words to use in his translations. His choice of words had a great influence on the way the English language developed. People all over Britain began to use the same words and this meant that it was easier for them to understand each other.

Caxton's work also encouraged more people to learn to read. As more books became available, there was a greater need to be able to read. Today, there are so many forms of printed information that the ability to read is essential.

Carrying messages

Hundreds of years ago people did not know what was happening outside their local area. The only information they had was from travellers or traders who went from one place to another. This was not reliable enough for the powerful rulers. They needed a swift and safe system of carrying messages to the distant parts of their lands. The first postal services consisted of systems of runners or riders carrying messages.

About 2000 years ago, the ancient Romans had a quick and reliable postal service covering the whole of their empire from Britain to Asia. At about the same time there were regular postal services in China and Persia. When the Venetian traveller Marco Polo arrived in China in 1275, he was amazed to learn how quickly letters could be sent all over China. However, only kings and rulers could use these services. Ordinary people still had to send messages by travellers or merchants.

Post for the people

In 1464, however, King Louis XI of France set up a postal service that could be used by anyone. He used messengers on horses and it was the person getting the letter who had to pay. Later, merchants, who often needed to send regular messages, organized their own postal services. The largest of these services was run by the Tasso family in Italy. They gradually extended their service to include all the many lands then under Austrian rule. Their service was so successful that it continued in parts of Germany until the 1850s.

In 1516 the English king Henry VIII appointed Brian Tukes to be Master of the Posts. Tukes organized a system of riders to carry messages around the

A postman on horseback. The Pony Express, which was started in 1860, delivered letters across North America with amazing speed. The riders had to stop and change horses every 16 kilometrs. The journey was sometimes dangerous. In this picture the rider is being chased by North American Indians.

country. In America, Benjamin Franklin, a famous inventor, was made Postmaster in 1775 and President George Washington helped find the best routes to speed the delivery of the post. In 1860 the Pony Express was started to take post to California, on the west coast of America. A letter from Missouri, in the east, took eight days to reach California by Pony Express.

▲ A 'penny black'

Postage stamps

Postage stamps were the idea of an Englishman called Rowland Hill. He thought that the person sending the letter should be the one to pay for the postage. The first stamps, called 'penny blacks', were used in Britain on 6 May 1840. They showed the head of Queen Victoria and cost one penny. They paid for a letter to be delivered anywhere in Britain. Postage stamps soon became very popular and there was a great increase in the number of letters sent by post.

The first regular airmail service was started in the United States in 1918. The aircraft carried post between Washington and New York. There are now airmail services throughout the world.

◀ **The inventor of postage stamps.** Before Rowland Hill introduced the postage stamp in 1840, postal charges were collected on delivery. Thanks to Hill, people no longer had to pay for receiving letters.

The birth of airmail. In 1918 the first airmail service was set up in the United States using War department aircraft and pilots. Here mail bags in Philadelphia, Pennsylvania, are transferred to an aircraft bound for New York.

Sending signals

One way of communicating with people is by sending them a signal. There are many ways to send simple signals. For example, a bonfire lit at the top of a hill can be seen a long way off. It is said that the ancient Greeks used a line of hill-top bonfires to send news of the fall of Troy to Argos in Greece, over 800 kilometres away, in just a few hours. In 1588, when the Spanish Armada was threatening England, a chain of bonfires was lit on hills across the country to let people know when the enemy fleet was in sight.

In a short time, the whole country knew that the Spaniards had arrived.

North American Indians used smoke signals to send messages. The clouds of smoke could be seen far away and warriors could understand the meaning of the signals from the number, colour and size of the clouds. Another effective way of signalling is by using mirrors. These can flash reflected sunlight over long distances. Armies used to use a device called a **heliograph**, which was made from mirrors, to send signals to their soldiers.

Messages in the sky. Different tribes of North American Indians used smoke signals to send messages to each other. They made the smoke by putting a wet blanket over a fire. When the blanket was lifted, a puff of smoke rose into the sky. The number, colour and size of the puffs all had special meanings.

Wartime signalling in the 1790s. This picture shows one of the semaphore signal towers built by Claude Chappé during the French Revolution. The arms of the tower were hand-operated. Different positions of the arms stood for letters and numbers.

Signalling with flags

If the sender and the receiver are only a short distance apart and can see each other, but cannot hear each other, they may use **semaphore** to send messages. A person holds his or her arms in different positions to indicate different letters of the alphabet. For instance, when the right arm is held straight up, and the left arm straight down, this

indicates the letter D. They often hold flags to make the signal more visible. Semaphore was used by navies to send messages from one ship to another and was very common before the days of radio and walkie-talkies.

Ships also used flags to send messages. There are 26 different flags standing for the different letters of the alphabet. These are arranged in different orders to send messages in code. There are also flags with special meanings. A yellow flag means 'We have sickness aboard'. A blue flag with a white square in the centre is called the Blue Peter. It means that the ship is about to leave port. These flags are still used because they are easily recognized and do not rely on verbal communication.

The signal towers

In the 1790s, during the French Revolution, a French merchant called Claude Chappé used a **semaphore telegraph** to send messages for the French army between the cities of Lille and Paris. Tall signalling towers were built between the two cities and messages were sent from tower to tower by moving metal arms on top of the towers to indicate letters and numbers. The arms could be moved to nearly 200 positions to convey messages. The system worked very well and a message could be sent to Paris, 240 kilometres away, in two minutes. Telegraphs like these were widely used in the early 1800s, until the **electric telegraph** was invented.

Messages by wire

U ntil about 200 hundred years ago, most communications relied either on a written message or on people being close enough to see or hear one another person. In 1752, the famous American scientist, Benjamin Franklin, discovered that electric **charges**, produced by rubbing silk on glass, could travel along metal wires. Many scientists tried to use this discovery to send messages along wires.

The power of electricity

It was Georges Lesage of Geneva in Switzerland who built the first **electric telegraph** in 1774. It worked like this. Wires were stretched between the person sending the message and the person getting the message. There was a separate wire for each letter of the alphabet. An electric charge was produced by rubbing a large glass ball with a silk cloth and this charge was applied to the end of the wire corresponding to the letter being sent. When the charge travelled to the other end of the wire, it made a small spark. This showed which letter was being sent, or transmitted.

Two discoveries helped make better telegraphs. In 1800 an Italian scientist called Alessandro Volta discovered how to make a **battery** for storing electricity. This could produce strong, steady currents of electricity. Then, in 1820 a Danish scientist called Hans Christian Oersted discovered that electricity sent along wires could move small magnets.

Magnetic messages

Two Englishmen, Charles Wheatstone and William Cooke, made use of these

The first electric telegraph, built by George Lesage in Geneva in 1774. The operator points an electrically-charged rod at a ball hanging from a wire. There is one ball for each letter of the alphabet. The electricity travels along the wire and a spark at the other end of the wire shows which letter was transmitted.

Spelling out messages. Wheatstone's telegraph had five needles that moved left or right as an electric current flowed along the telegraph line. When they moved, they spelt out a message by pointing to letters.

discoveries in 1837. They produced a new kind of telegraph that used electric batteries to produce strong electric currents, which were sent along the telegraph wires. At the receiving end of the telegraph, there were five small magnets. When an electric current flowed along the wires, the magnets turned to point at letters on a grid, spelling out the message being transmitted.

This new telegraph was built along a railway line near London and in 1845 it helped catch a murderer. John Tawell, who was wanted by the police, was spotted boarding a train. It was too late to stop the train so a message was sent by telegraph to the next station. Tawell was captured when the train arrived.

Charles Wheatstone set up the first electric telegraph in Britain in 1837. The telegraph sent messages along the railway line between two London stations.

Samuel Morse

All these early telegraphs were hard to use and they were slow to send messages because the operator had to keep looking to see which letter was being sent. In 1840 an American inventor called Samuel Morse developed an improved telegraph that overcame this problem. His system used a buzzer that made a sound and messages were sent as a code, using combinations of short and long buzzes to stand for the letters of the alphabet. This code was later called the **Morse Code**. Messages could be sent much faster in Morse Code. Samuel Morse's telegraph also printed out the message as it was being received.

Soon, telegraphs were being installed in many countries. By 1861 the east and west coasts of the United States were connected by telegraph. Strong wires, called cables, were laid on the bottom of the oceans so that telegraph messages could even be sent to different countries.

Speaking at a distance

Although the electric telegraph meant that messages could be sent between people far apart, they still could not have a conversation unless they were within earshot of each other. The invention that made this possible was the telephone. It is one of the most common means of communication we have today and it was invented by Alexander Graham Bell. He was born in Scotland in 1847 but went to live in Boston, in the United States, when he was 24.

In Boston, Bell taught in a school for deaf people. He decided to build an electrical device that would help deaf people to speak properly. Eventually he was joined by a young mechanic called Thomas Watson.

▲ **The world's first telephone receiver**, made by Alexander Graham Bell in 1875, looked very different from a modern telephone. It was made of a coil of wire and a magnetic arm. An electric current in the coil moved the magnet. This made vibrations that reproduced the sounds spoken into the receiver.

The first telephone call

At first, Bell and Watson worked on a kind of telegraph that could send more than one message at a time over a wire. Then Bell decided to build a machine to send sounds along a telegraph wire. His machine had two parts joined by wires. There was a **transmitter**, which sent the sounds, and a **receiver**, which picked up the sounds. The transmitter and receiver each contained a thin piece of metal, called a **diaphragm**, near an electric magnet. When someone spoke near the transmitter, the diaphragm inside vibrated, or moved back and forth. This movement made the magnet vibrate, causing an electric current in the wire to the receiver. The electric current made the diaphragm in the receiver move, making vibrations that sounded like the words that had been spoken into the transmitter.

In 1876 Bell sent his first telephone message from one room to another. The message was, 'Mr Watson, please come here – I want you.' He called his invention 'telephone' from two Greek words, tele meaning 'far-off' and phone

◄ **Telephone technology** has developed rapidly since the time of Bell. Today people can speak to each other even when they are travelling.

Alexander Graham Bell, the inventor of the telephone, made the first telephone call on the New York – Chicago service which was installed in 1892, six years after the Boston to New York line.

meaning 'sound'. His invention was going to transform the lives of millions of people.

Long-distance calls

The early telephones were not very efficient and users had to shout to be heard over even short distances. To begin with, there were so few telephones that hardly anyone saw the point in having one. In any case, in those days, many people could use their servants to carry messages much more cheaply.

However the telephone was soon improved. As a result of the work of the famous American inventor, Thomas Edison, the first long-distance telephone line was installed in 1884 between Boston and New York.

In 1889 the owner of a funeral parlour in Kansas City in the United States, called Almon Brown Strowger,

invented a system of automatic dialling for long-distance telephone calls. Before that people had to ask an operator to dial the number for them.

Telephones rapidly became an essential piece of equipment in homes and businesses around the world and today there are over 500 million telephones in use. Having a telephone also means that many people live less lonely or isolated lives. Many improvements have been made to telephones. People can carry portable telephones with them wherever they go. It is possible to connect a telephone to an answering machine so that you do not even have to listen to the call to receive a message. Telephones can pass messages between computers, and machines can be connected to the telephone to receive printed messages. Communications that once would have taken days can now be transmitted in minutes.

The great inventor

Many inventions have changed the way people live. The electric light meant that people did not have to rely on daylight to work. The moving picture brought a new form of entertainment and the **phonograph** made it possible for people to listen to music in their own homes instead of having to go to a concert hall. All these inventions were the work of one man, Thomas Alva Edison. He was born in 1847, in Ohio in the United States.

When Thomas Edison was young, he asked questions about everything he saw. He was so out of the ordinary that his teachers described him as 'addled', or crazy. His mother decided that such teachers were no use, and began to teach Thomas at home. He developed an interest in science, and refused to believe anything unless he could prove it for himself. Once, he tried to hatch goose eggs by sitting on them. On another occasion, he set fire to his father's barn to see what would happen!

First steps

At the age of 12, Edison went to work on the railways, selling groceries on a train that ran between Port Huron and Detroit. He started a newspaper that he printed in the luggage van of a train and he did chemical experiments on the train too. However, he was eventually thrown off one of the trains because he accidentally set fire to it.

During the American Civil War, Edison worked as a telegraph operator on the railway. His first invention was an electric vote recorder for use at elections. This was not a success, but he continued to come up with a great many other inventions that were much more successful.

Bright ideas

Edison's first successful invention was a **ticker tape** machine, a kind of telegraph that automatically printed out business information. It was used by traders to get up-to-date prices on various products. Edison made a lot of money

A great inventor. Thomas Edison's discoveries dramatically improved people's lives. This picture shows Edison at work in his laboratory. His invention factory employed 50 researchers.

▲ **Records go compact**. Sound recording has come a long way since the time of Edison. In 1887 a German, Emile Berliner, invented the flat disc record player or gramophone. In the early 1980s scientists developed the compact disc (CD). Wheras a record has a groove, a compact disc has thousands of tiny pits and bumps. Sound is produced as a laser beam passes over them.

from his machine. This enabled him to set up his own laboratory where he spent all his time inventing. The laboratory was at Menlo Park, New Jersey. He even kept a bed there and he rested only when he was too tired to carry on.

Edison improved Bell's telephone so that it could be used over long distances. Thanks to his work, the telephone could be used over distances of 160 kilometres. Before that it could not be used over a distance of more than a few kilometres.

In 1877, Edison invented the phonograph, a type of record player. He had earlier invented a microphone that would vibrate when sound fell on it and he added a needle to the microphone that scratched a groove in a thin sheet of tin foil as it vibrated. When he spoke into the microphone, the vibrating needle made a recording of the speech. The recorded speech could be played back by moving the needle through the recorded groove. The first record ever made was *Mary had a little lamb*.

▲ **Edison's first phonograph** made it possible to record sound and play it back. The first 'record' was a tin foil cylinder, but later wax cylinders were used. To make a recording, the cylinder was turned while words were spoken into the horn. The grooves in the cylinder were made by a needle that vibrated. Later, when the cylinder was turned, the grooves made the cylinder vibrate, reproducing the sounds.

Illuminating the world

Then, in 1879, Edison invented the electric light bulb. Electricity was passed through a thin strip, or **filament**, of burnt bamboo. When this happened, the filament glowed.

The electric light is used in many ways, not only to illuminate dark places. Lights are used in traffic signals, to guide aircraft, in lighthouses and to send messages. They are another essential part of modern communications. Edison was the greatest inventor of all time and was called 'the Wizard of Menlo Park'. When he died in 1931, he had made over a thousand important inventions.

The first photographers

One way of communicating information is by using a picture. Today, we use photographs to show what someone looks like or to describe a place. Although the principles of making a photograph have been known for hundreds of years, it was not until 1826 that the first photograph was produced. Before that, the only way of reproducing a picture, or **image**, was by painting it.

The simplest type of camera was invented as long as 900 years ago by the Arabs. It became known as a 'pin-hole' camera. It was a small, dark box with a tiny hole in one end to let in light. The light made a faint picture on the back of the box of any object or scene in front of the camera. About 400 years ago, Italian inventors found that the hole could be made larger if a piece of curved glass, called a **lens**, was placed in front of the hole. This produced a brighter, clearer image. There was, however, no way of making a permanent copy of this image.

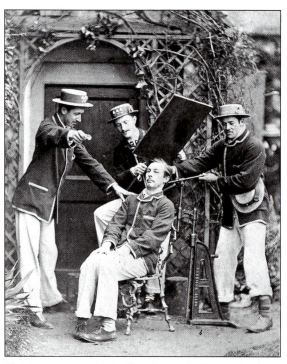

Holding a pose for half an hour. In the early days of photography it took such a long time to take a photograph that photographers had to use special supports to keep the person's head still.

Permanent pictures

The first photograph was taken in 1826. A Frenchman called Nicéphore Niepce produced a photograph using a pinhole camera with a lens fitted into one end. At the other end of the camera was a metal plate coated with a thin layer of bitumen and oil. Light entering the box through the lens fell onto the metal plate. After about eight hours, the bitumen became hard where the light was strongest. Niepce then washed off the soft bitumen and the hardened bitumen that remained formed a picture.

In 1837 another Frenchman, Louis Daguerre, invented a better process. It was much quicker and produced a sharper image. Daguerre used a metal plate coated with silver, which darkened when it was treated with chemicals and exposed to light. His photographs were known as **daguerreotypes**. It took half an hour to make a single daguerreotype and it was difficult to photograph people because they could not stay still for such a long time.

William Fox Talbot

In about 1835, an English photographer called William Fox Talbot made an important new discovery. He worked out how to make photographs on paper instead of on metal plates. Fox Talbot used special paper that darkened rapidly when light shone on it. This meant that photographs could be taken in only two minutes. He also discovered how to make copies of a photograph. This was done by shining light through a photograph made on transparent paper called **film**. He even took photographs through a microscope.

Modern photography began with Fox Talbot. Other people went on to develop his discoveries. In 1888 an American businessman called George Eastman made the first roll of film. He also introduced a small camera that was easy to use, and from then on it was possible for anyone to take a photograph.

A picture for the family album in 1873. Before photography was invented, only rich people could afford to have portraits painted. The invention of the camera gave many people the chance to own pictures of themselves and their families and friends. Photographs also enabled people to see for the first time exactly what distant places looked like.

Moving pictures

Moving pictures can show us more than a photograph can. They can show an action or event as it happens. The moving pictures we see in a cinema film are really a series of still pictures that are **projected** very rapidly. Each picture is slightly different from the one before and the pictures are flashed in front of our eyes one after the other. We see each picture for a short time only, and the pictures seem to join together and move smoothly. This happens because our eyes continue to see a picture for one-tenth of a second after it has been taken away. By the time the picture fades, another one has taken its place and our brain simply blends the pictures together.

The Zoetrope was a popular toy in the early 1800s. Around the inside of the cylinder is a strip of drawings of a man whose hat is blowing off. In each drawing the hat is slightly furthur away from his head. When you spin the cylinder and look through the slits, you seem to see a moving picture of the hat blowing off.

Tricks of light

In 1833 a popular toy called the zoetrope appeared. This was a cylinder with slits in the sides. When the cylinder was turned, moving figures could be seen through the slits. A series of figures, in various stages of movement, was drawn on the inside of the cylinder and as the cylinder moved round each one was seen in turn. This made it look as if the figures, not the cylinder, were moving.

In 1887 Thomas Edison, the famous American inventor, made a better machine. It was called the kinetograph. *Kine* is a Greek word meaning 'moving'. It had pictures on a length of photographic film. The film moved quickly through the machine when a handle was turned. Each image was seen for a short time as it flashed past an eyepiece. The kinetograph had one big disadvantage. Only one person could use it at a time.

The first film makers

Moving pictures were first shown on a screen in 1893 by a French scientist called Etienne Jules Marey. He used a simple **projector** known as a 'magic lantern', which shone pictures onto a screen or wall. The magic lantern normally projected pictures painted on glass slides but Marey passed a roll of film through the lantern, which produced pictures that moved.

Two French brothers, Auguste and Louis Lumière, became interested in making moving pictures after they had seen the kinetograph invented by Edison. In 1895 the brothers gave the first public cinema show in a café in Paris. Later, Louis showed his 'cinématographe' all round the world. He also taught other photographers how to make films. They were sent all over the world to record scenes from life. Some news films and short comedies were also made. Louis produced a total of about 1400 films before he retired in 1903.

The first cinemas

The early films were not in colour. They were in black and white, and they had no sound. Films with sound were first made in Germany in 1922. These films became known as the 'talkies'. The first colour films were not made until 1930 when a new process, called Technicolor, was used by Walt Disney in his colourful cartoons.

Films soon became one of the most popular forms of entertainment and communication. People began to go out to the cinema rather than providing their own entertainment in the home. Moving pictures were also used to record news events. These made it possible for people to see what was happening in other parts of the world.

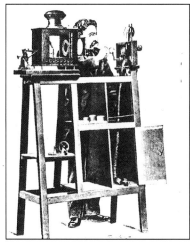

▲ **Projecting images**. This early cinema projector was used by the Lumière brothers. They gave the first public cinema show in 1895. Each film lasted about one minute. One film showed workers leaving their factory. Another film of an approaching train was so realistic that people ran away from the screen in terror.

▶ **A night at the cinema**. A packed British cinema shows that in 1909 films were already a popular form of entertainment. By 1912, Britain had about 4000 cinemas.

Invisible waves

How do radio and television carry messages? They do not use wires like the telephone, but a kind of wave that cannot be seen or heard. These waves spread out from the radio or television station in much the same way as ripples spread out across the water when a stone is dropped into a pond. They are ripples of electricity and magnetism that move through space and they are called **electromagnetic waves**. Radios and televisions also need a **transmitter** to send out the waves and a receiver to receive the waves. The **receiver** is, in fact, your radio or television set.

As early as 1873, a Scottish mathematician called James Clerk Maxwell worked out that electromagnetic waves must exist. He did this by using mathematics rather than by doing practical experiments. We now know that there are many different forms of electromagnetic waves. **Radio waves** are just one of them and light waves and X-rays are others. The only difference between these kinds of waves is the distance between their crests, or their highest points. This distance is known as the **wavelength**. Radio waves have long wavelengths, X-rays have short wavelengths.

James Clerk Maxwell discovered electromagnetic waves in 1873. This discovery eventually led to inventions such as the radio and television.

experiment. He connected two brass balls to an electrical supply. This device acted as a transmitter. He placed a device called a receiver a few metres away on the other side of the room. He then made a spark jump across the gap between the two balls in the transmitter. When he did this a faint spark was also seen in the gap in the equipment of the receiver. This spark was caused by electromagnetic waves that spread out from the transmitter when the spark jumped between the brass balls. The electromagnetic waves had travelled across the room. Hertz had succeeded in sending a signal.

Sending radio signals

A German scientist called Heinrich Hertz found out much more about these waves. In 1887 Hertz did an important

Communicating through air

Hertz's method of sending radio signals was improved by an English scientist called Oliver Lodge. Lodge was born in

▲ **Heinrich Hertz**

▲ **The first radio transmitter** was made by Heinrich Hertz in 1887. In the top part of this picture are two rods, with brass balls, marked A and B, at the ends. Using the electric supply shown in the bottom of the picture, Hertz sent a strong electric current to the balls. An electric spark jumped across the gap marked a – b. This spark caused electromagnetic waves to spread across the room, causing another spark in a receiver some distance away.

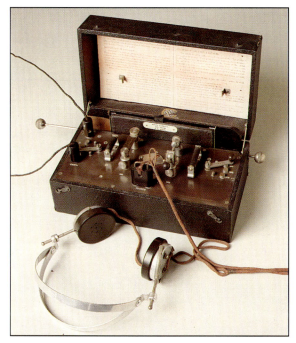

The first popular radios were called crystal sets. They received radio signals through a small piece of crystal. This was connected to the rest of the receiver by a thin wire, known as a 'cat's whisker'.

1851 and became the first professor of physics and mathematics at Liverpool University. In 1894 he succeeded in sending a radio signal a distance of 137 metres.

The discovery of electromagnetic waves and how to transmit and receive them made it possible for scientists and inventors to produce better ways of sending signals through the air. In 1900 Lodge discovered how to use a small piece of crystal to make a more sensitive receiver. These crystal sets were used for many years until more sensitive and sophisticated equipment was developed.

The beginning of the radio age

The person who showed that it was possible to send radio messages around the world was an Italian called Guglielmo Marconi. Although he was born in Italy, in 1874, it was in Britain that he became famous. Marconi began experimenting with radio waves when he heard of Lodge's experiments in 1894. He was soon able to ring an electric bell in one corner of his bedroom using radio waves sent from the other corner. He then decided to find a way of sending radio waves over greater distances.

Guglielmo Marconi with his transmitting and receiving apparatus. Marconi was known as 'the father of the wireless'. He found practical ways of communicating over long distances 'without wires', by using radio waves.

Early success in a foreign land

Marconi made a transmitter to send out radio waves and a receiver to collect the waves. To send the signal, he began using a piece of wire, called an **aerial**, trailing from a flying kite. This increased the distance one signal travelled. Soon he succeeded in sending signals over two and a half kilometres. However, no one in Italy seemed interested in his experiments, so he moved to Britain. His first success in Britain was to send a message from Wales to an island in the Bristol Channel. Then, in 1898, he became famous when he radioed medical bulletins about the Prince of Wales, who was ill in London, to Queen Victoria in her country home.

Transatlantic communication. On a windy day in 1901, Marconi and his assistants struggled to launch a kite, in Newfoundland, Canada. The kite carried a receiving aerial which detected the three dots forming the Morse Code 'S'. This had been sent from Cornwall, England, and was the first radio signal to be transmitted across the Atlantic.

A message across the sea

In 1901, Marconi tried to send a message across the Atlantic Ocean. Other scientists did not think radio waves would travel that far. They believed that radio waves would not be able to travel beyond the horizon. However, Marconi proved them wrong. He sent a signal from Cornwall in England, to Newfoundland in Canada, a distance of 3520 kilometres. The aerial on his receiving station was 122 metres long and held up by a kite. The message sent was the single letter 'S' in Morse code.

This success proved that radio could reach distant countries. In 1910 the British police used radio to capture a famous murderer called Henry Crippen.

He had escaped from England on a ship to Canada. However, the captain recognized Crippen and sent a radio message to the police in Britain. Detectives caught a faster ship to Canada, and arrested Crippen when he arrived.

A prize-winning inventor

Marconi was a successful businessman as well as a successful inventor. He founded a firm to make radios and other electrical goods. This company is now one of the major manufacturers in Britain. In 1909 Marconi was awarded the **Nobel Prize** for his discoveries. Marconi's pioneering work led to the widespread use of radio as a means of communication throughout the world.

Controlling the currents

At the same time as Marconi was experimenting with radio waves, other scientists were making important discoveries about **electronics**. Electronics is the science of controlling small electric currents, such as those found in radio receivers. Electronics is used to increase, or **amplify**, the weak currents in a radio so that they are strong enough to work a loudspeaker and produce sound.

Without electronics, there would be no radio, television or tape recorders in our homes. There would be no computers or traffic lights. Scientists would not have been able to develop radar, the use of radio waves to find the position of objects.

John Ambrose Fleming

The study of electronics began with an English professor called John Ambrose Fleming. Fleming was professor of electrical engineering at University College in London. He had helped to improve Edison's electric light. In 1904 Fleming was investigating an effect that Thomas Edison had first noticed in 1884.

He took an electric light bulb and inserted an extra wire through the glass. Then he connected this wire to an electric battery. An electric current flowed from the filament of the bulb to the wire. The device, which Fleming called a **diode valve**, could be used to control the flow of electricity in a circuit.

An electronics pioneer. John Ambrose Fleming pioneered the study of electronics. This picture shows him standing beside a dynamo, or generator, for producing steady electric currents.

The first electronic device. Fleming's diode valve was like an ordinary light bulb but with an extra wire inserted through the glass. Using the valve, scientists could build very sensitive radio receivers.

It was now possible to build very sensitive radio receivers using diodes.

Strengthening the signal

Lee de Forest was an American inventor who improved the diode valve. He was born in Iowa in 1873. As a young boy he was always experimenting with inventions. In 1907 he put a third wire, called a grid, into the bulb of a diode. He called his invention a **triode valve**. He found he could use the grid to control the amount of electricity passing through the bulb. When the grid was connected to a battery, the current flowing through the bulb was reduced.

By varying the amount of electricity applied to the grid, the electric current could be controlled. The triode valve was soon used to amplify, or strengthen, weak long-distance telephone calls and later it was used to strengthen radio signals.

The discoveries made by Fleming and de Forest meant that people far away from the transmitter could receive radio signals. In 1924 Marconi succeeded in sending a signal from Britain to Australia, on the other side of the world. The radio soon became one of the most important means of passing on information to large numbers of people.

Listening to an election broadcast in the 1930s. Hundreds of years ago, rulers sent important messages to the people by messengers who travelled from town to town. The invention of the radio meant that news, as well as entertainment, could be transmitted to many people quickly.

The beginnings of television

Who invented television? The answer is that no one person was the inventor and many people helped make television possible. One early pioneer was a German scientist named Ferdinand Braun. In 1897 he invented the **cathode-ray tube**, an electronic device that produces a small spot of light on a glass screen.

However, it was a Russian professor named Boris Rosing who first realized that this small spot of light could be used to form a picture. He managed to produce some simple pictures using the tube in about 1910. In 1923 another Russian-born scientist, Vladimir Zworykin, used the cathode-ray tube to make an electronic television camera, which he called the **iconoscope**. This could be pointed at a scene in order to show it as an image on a cathode-ray tube. This was the first simple television system.

John Logie Baird

A Scottish inventor called John Logie Baird discovered another way of producing television pictures. He saw no future in Zworykin's electronic camera. Instead, he used a rotating disc pierced with holes in his camera. As the disc rotated, a spot of light was moved across the scene that the camera was pointing at. An electric eye, or **photocell**, measured the brightness of the spot as it moved. Information about the brightness was transmitted, using radio waves, to the receiver, where the scene was put together again on a screen.

In October 1925 Baird succeeded in producing the first television picture of a person, a 15-year-old boy called Billy Taynton. Baird showed his television system in public for the first time in January 1926. He transmitted a small and blurred picture of a ventriloquist's dummy. In 1929 he began the world's first television service in London. At the time, there were only 100 television sets to receive the pictures.

A new age of communication

In the end, however, the iconoscope proved to be better than Baird's camera. In Britain, when the two cameras were tested side-by-side, Baird's camera

The basis of television. Inside every television set is a cathode ray tube. The picture is formed on the wide end of the tube by a beam of electricity which is shone onto the screen. As the beam moves across the screen, its brightness varies to produce the picture.

Sending a picture through space. John Logie Baird produced the first television picture of a person in 1925. This shows him with the transmitting disc he pioneered. As the disc rotated, light shone through the holes onto the scene being televised. The pattern of light produced was converted to an electrical signal and transmitted using radio waves. The receiver converted the electrical signal back into a picture using a cathode ray tube. Unfortunately, Baird's system gave poor quality pictures and soon went out of use.

performed poorly. It had to be bolted to the floor because it kept vibrating and gallons of water were needed to stop it overheating. The pictures it produced were blurred and faint.

Before long, all television stations were using the iconoscope electronic camera and Baird's system went out of use. The first all-electronic television services started in Germany in 1935, and in America in 1939. These early services could only transmit pictures in black and white.

The colour television camera was perfected in the United States in 1953. It split the light from the scene being televised, or filmed, into three colours, red, blue and green. A signal representing each colour was transmitted to the receiver, where the colours of the original scene were reproduced by mixing the red, blue and green signals. Soon, colour television programmes were being seen in many countries.

Calculating machines

People have always needed to count and calculate. Farmers need to count their cattle, and merchants need to calculate the price of their goods. Early people used to count on their fingers or scratch marks on the ground. The Romans used pebbles called calculi for counting. This is where we get our word 'calculate' from.

Over 4500 years ago, the Chinese or the Babylonians invented a device for making calculations called an **abacus**. This is a frame with vertical rods strung with beads. Each bead on the first rod is worth one, on the next rod a bead is worth 10, and so on. Calculations are done by moving the beads up and down the rods.

The first mechanical machine for calculating was made by a Frenchman called Blaise Pascal in 1642. From an

▲ **The first mechanical calculator**. This machine, called a pascaline, was invented by Blaise Pascal in 1642 when he was only 19. It could add, subtract and even multiply.

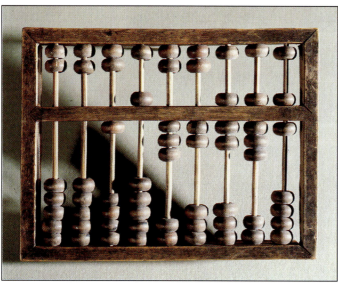

An early calculating device. To calculate on this nineteenth-century Chinese abacus, beads are moved up or down to the central bar. Beads in the upper section count as five units each. Those in the lower section count as one unit each.

Blaise Pascal

early age, Pascal had shown that he was a genius, especially in mathematics. He made his first calculating machine when he was only 19. This was a box full of toothed wheels, or cogs, and numbers were added together by turning a series of dials on the front. As the dials turned, the cogs inside turned too. The total of the numbers dialled was shown on the front. The machine could also multiply numbers by a complicated sequence of additions. Pascal's idea of using cogwheels to add numbers was used in calculating machines for over 300 years.

The father of the computer

Charles Babbage was a brilliant man who was a professor of mathematics at Cambridge University in England for 16 years. He was born in 1792 in Devon, in the south west of England. He loved to spot errors in others people's work and to tell very famous people about their mistakes! In 1822 he designed a calculating machine called the 'Difference Engine' to do scientific calculations. It used toothed wheels on shafts turned by a crank, or handle. He spent over 10 years trying to build it but because he was always changing it and trying to improve it, he never got it finished.

Then Babbage had an even better idea. He decided to build a machine that could do a wide range of calculations by following instructions supplied by the user. He called this machine the 'Analytical Engine'. It was designed to have a **memory** that would record the

Charles Babbage was the man who almost invented computers. Throughout his life, Babbage tried to design a machine that would do complex calculations. Although his machines were never built, today's electronic computers owe a lot to his ideas.

instructions and the results of calculations on punched cards, and to have a powerful arithmetic unit to do the calculations. Unfortunately, however, Babbage was unsuccessful again. He died in 1871 and the Analytical Engine was never completed.

Although Babbage never saw his inventions in use, his ideas were used much later, in the 1940s, when the **computer** was developed. Modern computers are given a set of instructions, called a **program**, to follow and they have a memory and an arithmetic unit like Babbage's machine. Scientists now consider Babbage's ideas to be so important that they are building a real, working Difference Engine to be displayed at the Science Museum in London.

The first computer

Alan Turing was a genius. He was born in England in 1912 and showed an early talent for mathematics. As soon as he could read and write, he began his study of mathematics and science. He won many school prizes and then a scholarship to Cambridge University in England. While at university, he acquired a reputation for strange behaviour. He preferred to tell the time from the stars rather than wear a watch and he wore a gas mask to ease his hay fever.

The Turing machine

At the age of 24, Turing designed an imaginary machine that could do complicated calculations. Information would be fed into the machine on a paper tape, divided into squares. Each square would either be marked with a cross or left blank. The machine could either erase a cross or put a cross in a blank square according to the **program** stored in its memory. Turing showed that such a simple machine could do every sort of calculation. It was called the Turing machine and was, in some ways very like a modern computer.

'Colossus' the code-breaker

In 1939 Britain and Germany were at war and Turing went to work in a secret Government centre at Bletchley Park, Buckinghamshire. His ideas were used to build a huge machine called 'Colossus'.

Decoding secret messages was the job of this giant electronic computer during the Second World War. The first computers were so big that they often filled a whole room.

This machine was needed to break the German codes and to decode secret messages. Fast machines were needed to crack the codes because the German codes were changed each day.

The Colossus machine had 2000 triode valves. Messages to be decoded were fed into the machine on paper tape at high speed. The machine worked by replacing each letter in a signal with another letter. This was done many different times until a pattern began to emerge. Once a common phrase in the signal had been partly decoded in this way, the code-breakers could work out the rest of the message.

Towards the end of the war, Turing was asked to draw up plans for a computer based on his ideas. It was to be called ACE, or Automatic Computing Engine. The ACE was named partly after Babbage's 'Analytical Engine' and, like Babbage's machine, it took a long time to build. Turing became frustrated by the delays so he resigned and moved to Manchester. There he helped to build the first real computers to be produced in Britain. He also started to study the question, 'Can machines think?'. He worked out a test, still called the Turing Test, that is used to decide if a machine can be considered to be intelligent. Unfortunately, Turing became depressed because no one seemed able to understand his eccentric ways, and in 1954 he committed suicide. Nevertheless, his ideas were very important to the development of computers.

▼ **Playing with computers**. Today's computers are so sophisticated that they can play complex games like chess. A chess computer works by examining every possible move that could arise after its opponant moves. It can examine millions of possible moves in a second, and look many moves ahead to locate dangers.

▲ **A computer pioneer**. In the 1950s Alan Turing (the man standing in the picture) helped to build the first real computers in Britain. He also explored ways of programming machines to 'think'.

35

Towards the computer age

The first all-electronic computer was built in 1946, by John Mauchly and Presper Eckert. It was developed in Pennsylvania, in the United States, and was used by the army to help calculate the flight of artillery shells. This Electronic Numerical Integrator and Computer, or ENIAC, weighed 30 tonnes and contained 18 000 valves.

ENIAC occupied a large room and its valves were so short-lived that the computer would not run for more than two minutes without a valve failing! Despite this, it was a great success. ENIAC was 'faster than thought', wrote one enthusiastic newspaper reporter.

However, in order to alter its program, engineers had to completely change the wiring. This took hours or even days.

John von Neumann

One of the scientists working on ENIAC was John von Neumann. He was born in 1903, in Budapest in Hungary. He was a brilliant mathematician and by the time he was 25 years old he had obtained three university degrees. He liked to amaze his friends by doing difficult calculations in his head. Yet he was forgetful about other things when he was concentrating on scientific problems. Sometimes, when he was travelling, he

The first electronic computer, ENIAC, was developed in 1946. In contrast to today's computers, ENIAC took up a whole room, measuring 9 metres by 30 metres. It produced so much heat that the temperature of the room sometimes reached 50° C.

▲ **A brilliant mathematician**. John von Neumann designed a computer that could store its programs in a memory. Since the program could be changed easily, von Neuman's computer could be instructed to do many different tasks. It was the first all-purpose computing machine.

would forget where he was going and would have to telephone his office to find out.

At the start of the Second World War in 1939, von Neumann moved to the United States. There he joined the team of scientists who were trying to develop an atomic bomb. When he learned about the ENIAC computer, he immediately realized its importance and he joined the ENIAC team.

Von Neumann saw that it would be much better if computer instructions could be changed easily. He designed a computer that could memorize all its instructions. This meant that the engineer just had to tell the computer which program, or set of instructions, to use instead of having to change its wiring. He also made other improvements to computer design, and planned the main features of a modern computer.

Commercial computers arrive

In 1948 two British scientists called Frederic Williams and Tom Kilburn built the first computer to von Neumann's design. It was called the *Mark 1*, and it was built in Manchester, England. It stored its program in a **memory** and could do all kinds of calculations.

At this time, many scientists were building computers. John Mauchly and Presper Eckert built a computer, based on ENIAC, for business use. It was called UNIVAC, the Universal Automatic Computer. In 1950 UNIVAC became the first computer to be mass produced.

Today, computers are found in almost every business as well as in the home. They do routine jobs more accurately and more rapidly than people and they are able to store and evaluate an enormous amount of information. Computers can be linked together via the telephone so that information can be passed from one computer to another. Computers are used to fly aircraft, to control complicated transport systems and to operate satellites far out in space.

◄ **Computerized communication**. Today, computers are at the heart of every business. At this telephone control service in the United States, there are 72 computer screens. The software can do tasks such as working out the most efficient rate for long distance calls.

From valves to transitors

At the beginning of the electronic age, electrical signals were controlled by valves. The electronic valves used in the 1940s were not ideal. They were made from thin glass bulbs, with a hot filament inside. They were easy to break, were too large, and used too much electricity. They also burned out easily. An early computer using valves, like ENIAC, produced as much heat as 200 electric heaters.

The solution to these problems was to use materials called **semiconductors**. These materials could **conduct**, or carry, electricity without needing a heated filament. However, they do not do so as well as metals and so do not get as hot. One semiconductor material was a mineral called galena. It had been used in crystal set radios in the early 1900s. Unfortunately, the crystal set radio was unreliable, and it could not amplify the strength of signals. This meant it could not be used over very long distances.

The men who invented transistors. The American scientists, William Shockley, Walter Brattain and John Bardeen, won the Nobel Prize for their work in electronics. Their small and efficient transistors replaced the big, short-lived electronic valves.

The first transistor

In 1947 three American scientists, John Bardeen, William Shockley and Walter Brattain, discovered how to make a semiconductor **amplifier**. They all worked in the research laboratory of a large telephone company in New Jersey. William Shockley was the leader of the team. He was a 35-year-old Englishman who had spent most of his life in California. Walter Brattain had 16 years' research experience, and John Bardeen was a brilliant young scientist.

The team's invention was called the **transistor**. It was made up of a small piece of a semiconductor called **germanium** with three fine wires attached to it. It worked like a triode valve. When an electric current was passed through the wires, the current

Pocket-sized radios. The invention of the silicon transistor meant that much smaller radios and televisions could be made. The personal stereo, developed in the 1980s lets you take your music with you wherever you go.

was increased, or amplified.

The next breakthrough was the discovery that by introducing impurities into the material of the semiconductor different types of semiconductor could be produced. This process was called **doping**. In 1951, Shockley showed that when layers of different semiconductors were sandwiched together an even more reliable transistor was produced. These transistors could do everything a valve could, but were smaller, used less electricity and were more reliable. In 1956, the three scientists were awarded the Nobel Prize for their discovery.

Making transistors from sand

In 1954 Gorden Teal, an American electronics engineer, perfected a transistor made out of **silicon**. Silicon is found in sand and is much cheaper than germanium, which costs more than gold. The silicon transistor was not only cheap – it could also be made very small. It was reliable and was soon being widely used in radios, television receivers and space rockets.

The development of cheap, small transistors made it possible to mass-produce cheap radios and televisions which most people could afford. The availability of these cheap forms of communication has had an important influence on the lives of millions of people. We can receive information about events while they are happening or soon afterwards and people living in remote areas can be linked to the outside world.

The incredible silicon chip

During the early 1950s, transistors were mass-produced for use in radios, televisions and other electronic devices. A large number of transistors could be produced at the same time from a sheet of silicon. However, the transistors then had to be cut from the silicon sheet and wired together to form an electronic **circuit**. Some space engineers thought that this circuit took up too much room. They wanted very small circuits that they could cram into space rockets where there was very little room.

In 1952 a British engineer called Geoffrey Dummer suggested a way of making very small circuits. His idea was to make a whole circuit, including the connecting wires, on a piece of silicon. This sort of circuit became known as an **integrated circuit**, or chip. Unfortunately, however, Dummer never managed to build one.

Working in miniature

An American called Jack St Clair Kilby succeeded where Dummer had failed. He was working for an electronics firm in Texas and, without knowing about Dummer's idea, he decided to build a complete electronic circuit on a single piece of germanium.

In July 1958, Kilby made his first

A circular slice of silicon, or a 'wafer', contains hundreds of rectangular integrated circuits. The circuits, or chips, are constructed on the wafer and then cut from it. Just one of these chips contains hundreds of transistors. (This picture has been greatly enlarged and has been coloured to show the separate components more clearly).

▲ **The designer of the integrated circuit**, or chip, was Jack Kilby, an American engineer. He put a number of transistors on one tiny piece of germanium to form a complete electrical circuit. This small circuit meant that smaller and lighter computers could be made.

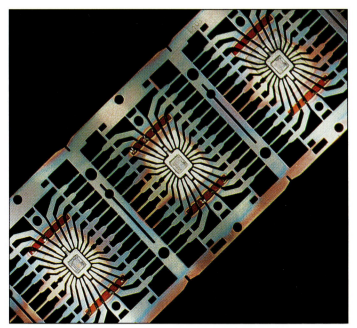

Microchips. This enlarged picture shows three microchips – the tiny rectangles in the centre of each unit. Surrounding each chip are the connections needed to attach it to electrical wires in a computer.

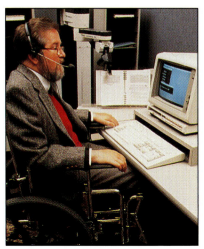

▲ **The microchip at work**. Thanks to the microchip, this disabled man has easy access to information. His computer contains a microchip which is controlled by voice commands. The computer moves a robot arm to load disks and retrieve the information stored on them.

integrated circuit. It was built on a piece of germanium that was only about as big as a match head. It had five components joined together by fine wires that were soldered on. It was not very neat, but it worked. Kilby convinced his boss that his invention was important, and the company began making integrated circuits. To show how useful they were, they built a computer using integrated circuits. This was very much smaller, and used less electricity, than any other computer.

One chip does everything

In 1971 Ted Hoff, a 34-year-old American engineer from California, went even further. He was working on a new

design for a calculator. The design needed 12 integrated circuits that had to be wired together to make the calculator. Hoff simplified this design by making a new chip, called a **microprocessor**.

The microprocessor could do the job of several chips. It had 2250 transistors built on a single chip. It was actually a computer on a chip because it could do arithmetic and make simple decisions. Its parts were arranged so that it could be programmed to carry out many different jobs.

Today, microprocessors are built into cars, cameras, spacecraft and computer-assisted typewriters called **wordprocessors**. They are the 'brain' behind a home computer, or **microcomputer**.

Communications in space

A **satellite** is a small object that circles, or orbits, around a larger object. The Moon is a satellite of the Earth. An artificial satellite is a man-made device that orbits the Earth. Its speed is so great that it never falls back to the ground and it must be launched into space by a rocket.

The first artificial satellite was called *Sputnik 1*. It was launched on 4 October 1957 by the Soviet Union. *Sputnik* travelled around the world in about 100 minutes, sending out radio messages as it went. This showed that satellites could be used for communications. Today there are hundreds of satellites in space, beaming radio messages and television programmes to all parts of the world. They are called **communications satellites**.

Echo and *Telstar*

The first satellite to send television programmes was a large balloon, called *Echo 1*, that was launched into orbit in 1960. The balloon acted as a huge mirror. It reflected television signals transmitted from the ground and sent them to a different place on the Earth. In 1962 a satellite called *Telstar* was launched. It travelled around the Earth in a couple of hours, at a height of about 400 kilometres. *Telstar* could receive a radio message from Earth and strengthen it before sending it back. The first television signals across the Atlantic Ocean were sent using *Telstar*.

Making fiction into fact. The author Arthur C. Clarke had the idea for a geostationary satellite in 1954. A geostationary satellite circles the Earth at the same speed as the Earth spins round. This means that it is always in the same position above the Equator and looks as if it is not moving. This picture shows Clarke in front of his own satellite receiving dish. He uses the dish to send stories from his home in Sri Lanka to England for printing.

Orbiting at the same speed

In 1954 Arthur C. Clarke, a famous writer of science fiction stories, had a brilliant idea. He saw that if a satellite could be placed in the correct orbit above the Equator, it could be made to circle the Earth at exactly the same speed as the Earth spins round. This

▶ Communications in space.
This is an artist's impression
of a communications satellite
orbiting the Earth. Using a
circle of satellites like this
one, we can now send words
and pictures right round the
world.

▼ A link with distant places.
This picture shows a satellite
dish at a receiving station in
the United States. A
communications satellite
receives a message in one
country, strengthens it, and
sends it to another part of
the world. Most telephone
calls between distant
countries are now sent using
satellites.

meant that the satellite would always be
in the same position above the Equator.
To do this the satellite would have to be
in an orbit at a height of 35 900
kilometres. This type of satellite is called
a **geostationary satellite**, which means
that it appears not to move.

Clarke believed that, with a few
geostationary satellites placed in the right
spots, messages could be sent from one
satellite to another, until the message had
passed right around the world. In April
1965 a satellite called *Early Bird* was put
into a geostationary orbit above the
Atlantic Ocean. In 1967 a second
geostationary satellite was in orbit above
the Pacific Ocean, and, in 1969, a third
satellite was placed over the Indian
Ocean. These satellites can carry over
12 000 telephone conversations, or 50
television programmes, at the same time.
They can carry messages to the far side
of the Earth in seconds.

The dream of being able to
communicate instantly with any part of
the world, shared by the pioneers of
communications over the ages, has
finally become a reality. It is also
possible to communicate with satellites
and space probes in outer space.
Science-fiction is rapidly becoming
science-fact.

Time chart

Date	Pioneer	Achievement
About 3500BC	The Sumerians	Use pictographs, or picture writing
About 3000 BC	The Persians and Babylonians	Develop cuneiform writing
About 3000BC	The Egyptians	Use hieroglyphs
About 1300BC		First alphabet developed at Ugarit in Syria
About 1000BC	The Greeks	Adopt the Ugarit alphabet
About 400BC	The Romans	Develop the Roman alphabet
About 50BC	The Romans	Use a postal service
868AD	The Chinese	Produce the first printed book
1040	The Chinese	Develop moveable type
1445	Johannes Gutenberg	Develops moveable type in Europe
1464	Louis XI	Sets up a postal service in France
1476	William Caxton	Introduces printing to England
1516	Brian Tukes	Appointed Master of Posts in England
1642	Blaise Pascal	Makes the first mechanical calculating machine
1774	Georges Lesage	Builds a simple electric telegraph
1775	Benjamin Franklin	Made Postmaster in the United States
1793	Claude Chappé	Invents the semaphore telegraph
1820	Hans Christian Oersted	Discovers the magnetic effect of an electric current
1826	Nicéphore Niepce	Takes the first photograph
1822	Charles Babbage	Designs the 'Difference Engine'
1834	Charles Babbage	Designs the 'Analytical Engine'
1835	William Fox Talbot	Makes photographs on paper
1837	Charles Wheatstone and William Cooke	Build the magnetic telegraph
1837	Louis Daguerre	Improves the photographic process
1840	Rowland Hill	Introduces the first postal stamp
1840	Samuel Morse	Introduces the Morse Code and improves the telegraph
1873	James Clerk Maxwell	Predicts the existence of electromagnetic waves

Date	Pioneer	Achievement
1876	Alexander Graham Bell	Invents the telephone
1877	Thomas Edison	Invents the phonograph
1884		The first long-distance telephone line is installed
1887	Heinrich Hertz	Discovers radio waves
1887	Thomas Edison	Invents the kinetograph
1888	George Eastman	Introduces photographic film
1894	Oliver Lodge	Sends a radio signal 137 metres
1895	Lumière brothers	Give the first cinema show
1897	Ferdinand Braun	Invents the cathode-ray tube
1901	Guglielmo Marconi	Sends a radio signal across the Atlantic Ocean
1904	John Ambrose Fleming	Invents the diode valve
1907	Lee de Forest	Invents the triode valve
1922		The first sound film is introduced
1923	Vladimir Zworykin	Invents the electronic television camera
1924	Guglielmo Marconi	Sends a radio signal from England to Australia
1925	John Logie Baird	Produces a mechanical television system
1929		The world's first television service begins in London
1930		Colour films are introduced
1946	John Mauchly and Presper Eckert	Build the first all-electronic computer, ENIAC
1947	John Bardeen, William Shockley and Walter Brattain	Invent the transistor
1948	Frederic Williams and Tom Kilburn	Build the first modern computer
1950	John Mauchly and Presper Eckert	Build the first mass-produced computer, UNIVAC
1953		Colour television is perfected in the United States
1954	Gordon Teale	Invents the silicon transistor
1954	Arthur C. Clarke	Suggests the use of geostationary satellites
1958	Jack Kilby	Produces the first integrated circuit
1960		The first communications satellite, *Echo 1*, is launched
1965		The first geostationary satellite is launched
1971	Tedd Hoff	Invents the microprocessor

Glossary

abacus: a calculating device that uses beads on rods to stand for numbers

aerial: a long wire used to transmit or receive radio or television signals. Television sets are connected to an aerial on the roof of a building

alphabet: the letters used to represent the sounds of a language

amplifier: an electronic device that strengthen radio or television signals

amplify: to make a signal, such as a radio signal, stronger

battery: a device that uses chemicals to produce or store electricity

biology: the study of living things

biologist: a scientist who studies living things

cathode-ray tube: a glass tube used in television. It has one flat end on which spots of light are produced to form a picture

character: a symbol used as part of a system of writing

chemist: a person who studies chemistry

chemistry: the science that studies what substances are made of, how they react together, and what properties they have

circuit: an electrical pathway made of wires. Electric circuits are found in radios and television sets

communications satellite: a space machine that moves around the Earth very high above the ground. It is used to pass messages around the world

computer: an electronic device that can calculate very quickly and accurately. It follows a set of instructions, or program, held in its memory

conduct: to allow electricity or heat to flow through a substance, such as metal

cuneiform: a form of writing used by the Persians and Babylonians about 5000 years ago

daguerreotype: an early type of photograph, invented by Louis Daguerre

diaphragm: a vibrating disc in a telephone that picks up sounds

diode valve: an electronic device for controlling electric current. It conducts electricity in one direction only

doping: adding small amounts of chemicals to a pure semiconductor to help electricity flow more easily

electric telegraph: a device for sending messages along wires using electricity

electromagnetic wave: a ripple of electricity and magnetism that can travel through empty space. Light, X-rays and radio waves are all electromagnetic waves

electronics: the science of using small electrical currents in devices such as radios and television sets

experiment: a test carried out in controlled conditions to discover something new or to prove that an idea is correct

filament: a thin strand of wire inside a light bulb that glows when an electric current is passed through it

film: a thin sheet of material used in a camera. It is sensitive to light

geostationary satellite: a space machine with an orbit that keeps in time with the spinning Earth below. It seems to stay in one place in the sky

germanium: a semiconductor material used in integrated circuits

heliograph: a machine used for signalling, using mirrors that reflect light from the sun

hieroglyphs: a form of picture writing used by the ancient Egyptians about 5000 years ago

iconoscope: an early type of television camera

image: a picture formed by a lens or mirror

integrated circuit: an electronic circuit built on a very small piece of semiconductor material

lens: a piece of glass with curved surfaces that is able to bend light beams

memory: the part of a computer that stores information

microcomputer: a small computer

microprocessor: an integrated circuit that can be programmed to do arithmetic and make simple decisions

microwave: an electromagnetic wave with a wavelength between 50 centimetres and 1 millimetre, which has an extremely high frequency

Morse Code: a code used to send messages by radio and telegraph. It uses combinations of dots and dashes to stand for letters

moveable type: printing type made up of single letters on separate pieces of metal that can be moved about

Nobel Prize: an annual prize awarded to scientists who have made important discoveries in physics, chemistry and medicine and to writers, economists and workers for peace

phonograph: an early name for the gramophone or record-player. The first ones used a cylinder instead of a flat disc

photocell: or photoelectric cell. A device in an electric circuit, which produces an electronic current when light passes through it

physics: the science that studies matter, the forces of nature and the different forms of energy, such as heat, light and motion

physicist: a person who studies physics

pictograph: a symbol representing a word or sound

printing block: a plate of wood or metal used in printing

printing press: the machine that presses the paper onto the inked type during printing

program: the set of instructions given to a computer

project: to make an image appear on a screen by shining light through a piece of film

radio wave: electromagnetic waves used to carry messages

receiver: a device for receiving radio, television or similar signals

satellite: a small body that circles, or orbits, a larger one. A communications satellite orbits the Earth and is used to pass messages between countries

science: the study of the way the world works, by using experiments and careful observation

semaphore: a system of sending signals by holding the arms or flags in different positions

semaphore telegraph: a system of sending signals by moving mechanical levers on towers

semiconductor: a material that can conduct electricity, but not as well as a metal

silicon: a semiconductor material used in integrated circuits. It is found naturally in sand

technology: the ways in which the discoveries of science may be used to make machines

telecommunications: ways of sending messages using devices such as the telephone, radio or television

ticker-tape: paper tape that is printed automatically from a telegraph system. It records business information

transmitter: a device for sending out radio, television or similar signals. To transmit means to 'send across' or to 'pass on'

transistor: an electronic device made of semiconductor material that can amplify an electrical signal

triode valve: an electronic device with three terminals that can amplify an electrical signal

valve: an electronic device consisting of a glass bulb with terminals attached, used to control electric currents

wavelength: the distance between two crests of an electromagnetic wave or sound wave

wordprocessor: an electronic typewriter. It can be used to store and change text using a computer program

X-ray: a type of electromagnetic wave that can pass through some materials

Index